101 WRITING PROMPTS
FOR GRADES K-2

BOOKS FOR YOUNG WRITERS FROM RED WOLF PRESS:

Story Starters:
101 Story Starters for Little Kids by Maisy Day
101 Story Starters for Kids by Dena McMurdie
101 Story Starters for Teens by Maisy Day

Writing Prompts:
101 Writing Prompts for High School by Mark Trevor
101 Writing Prompts for Middle School by Mark Trevor
101 Writing Prompts for Grades 3-5 by Mark Trevor
101 Writing Prompts for Grades K-2 by Mark Trevor

Poetry Writing:
Giggle-Worthy Poem Prompts for Kids by Mike Downs and Sandra K. Athans

101 WRITING PROMPTS FOR GRADES K-2

by
Mark
Trevor

RED WOLF
PRESS

RED WOLF PRESS

ISBN: 978-1-955731-12-6

Copyright © 2025 Red Wolf Press. All rights reserved.

Published by Red Wolf Press.

Interior design and cover design by Dena McMurdie.

Cover art by yusufdemirci, jannystockphoto, and MisterElements.

First printing, June 2025.

IMAGE CREDITS:
Front cover: all images depositphotos—background, hands, pencil, wood grain: yusufdemirci, doodles: MisterElements, post-it note: jannystockphoto.
Back cover: all images depositphotos—woodgrain, plant, pencil, post-it notes, paper clips: yusufdemirci, doodle: MisterElements.
Interior: All images depositphotos. **Page 5-26:** bear, child walking dog, flowers, pencil, exercise, fishing, nap, watching TV, exercise equipment, reading with mom, visiting friends, planting flowers, bear, scissors, dog, cat, children with apple, clock, teacher with children, teacher reading to class, happy girl, teacher and children at chalkboard, friends at table, teacher reading stories, teacher and classroom, boy on slide, boy laying under palm tree, boy building sand castle, seashells, children swimming in ocean, birthday party, birthday guests, eating ice cream, birthday with friends, boy on slide, girl on swings, learning to ride a bike, play in the sandbox: Katerina_Dav, **27:** elephant, tiger, giraffe, skunk: funnyclay, **28-30:** chickens, fish, cats, reading books, watching TV, playing with toys, playing with friends, riding a bike, boy on slide, kids swimming in ocean, kids rollerblading: Katerina_Dav, **31:** chicks: Sabelskaya, **32-49:** child watering garden, building a snowman, fox, owl, deer, rabbit, girl with umbrella, boy under palm tree, boy with pumpkin, boy on skis, boy in leaves, girl in princess costume, boys outside school, mouse, family watching TV, children riding pencil, boy reading, dogs playing, children with pets, astronaut, doctor, musician, girl drawing: Katerina_Dav, **50:** drumstick, french fries, ice cream, pizza: Polina_Sova, **51-53:** virtual reality, hide-and-seek, boy with butterfly, boy crying with girl comforting: Katerina_Dav, **54:** lost tooth: ronleishman, **55:** bee with flowers, giraffe: Katerina_Dav, **56:** lion, tiger: virinaflora, **57:** boy and genie: ronleishman, **58:** boy crafting, girl playing tennis, boy reading, musician: Katerina_Dav, **59:** child in movie theater seat, child on swing: ronleishman, **60-73:** teacher with group of children, children rollerblading, submarine, boy sleeping, girl with cat, familyl picnic, children with grandmother, building snowman, skating, sledding, skiing, fish, duck, turtle, fishing, boy with bike, girl reading by window, friends at school: Katerina_Dav, **74:** dolphin, shark: izakowski, **75-81:** santa, child with bunny ears, fireworks, mummy, child with award, child reading, child with lightbulb, parent and child exercising, child sleeping, parent and child cooking, child with water, boy with bike, fishing, reading, cooking: Katerina_Dav, **82:** cookie jar, popcorn bucket: ronleishman, **84-103:** boy walking dog, girls playing with ball, boys with soccer ball and skateboard, family in car, children with snowman, bee, butterfly, friends at school, car, airplane, family camping, boy on slide, girls playing with ball, children with backpacks and apple, children with dragon, children on train, children with emotions, happy children dancing with cat, family watching TV: Katerina_Dav, **104:** money: mhatzapa, **105-109:** astronauts, lizard, bird: Katerina_Dav.

TABLE OF CONTENTS

OVERVIEW

Reading and writing are the cornerstones of a child's education, and students should learn these skills as early as possible. I link these two areas because they are deeply intertwined and depend on each other.

Of the two skills, I've noticed that most students find writing more challenging. Even strong readers often need help to express their ideas on paper. However, good writing is essential for success in middle school, high school, and beyond. For this reason, becoming proficient writers when they are young will benefit students as they get older.

That's why I created this book of fun writing prompts—to help spark children's imaginations and get words on the page.

This book contains over 100 engaging writing and drawing prompts for students in grades K-2. These prompts will encourage students to put their imaginations and budding writing skills to use. You'll find plenty of topics children like to write about, such as themselves, family, friends, pets, and a few that allow their imaginations to run wild.

I am honored that you chose my book, and I hope it will be a valuable resource.

MARK TREVOR

HOW TO USE THIS BOOK

I constructed these writing prompts for each grade level and designed them to grow more challenging as students progress. The kindergarten prompts offer the most guidance to young writers, while the first and second-grade prompts allow them more freedom to express their ideas.

The breakdown below describes the general requirements and expectations at each level.

Kindergarten:

When kids start kindergarten, they learn letters and their corresponding sounds. They also learn to write words and use simple punctuation, like periods. The kindergarten prompts in this book are about familiar topics, like families, school, and animals. Many of the prompts have a word bank to help students get started.

Students will use sight words and complete fill-in-the-blank activities using basic nouns, verbs, and adjectives.

These prompts also introduce students to academic concepts such as shapes, numbers, and rhyme, and higher-level skills such as sequencing and providing one or two supporting details.

First Grade:

By first grade, most students can write legibly and understand phonics. They can also understand the elements of a simple sentence, such as a subject and a verb.

The prompts in this section ask kids to write about their feelings, interests, experiences, and opinions. They will write longer, more creative answers, like short poems or stories.

Second Grade:

By second grade, students have a more extensive vocabulary and more experience putting ideas down on paper. The prompts for this grade encourage students to write responses of 3-4 sentences.

These prompts build on familiar concepts and ask students to make comparisons, share opinions, and expand their creativity with longer poems and narratives.

TIPS FOR PARENTS

Read aloud with your child.

Studies show that this simple task has a powerful impact on a child's language development. Bedtime is the perfect opportunity for reading together.

Visit libraries and stores where children can explore books and bring them home.

As I mentioned earlier, the connection between reading and writing is undeniable. As a teacher of over 20 years, I can attest that the best writers are those who read often.

Give your child a blank book or journal.

Let them use the book to doodle, draw cartoons, or practice writing. It will improve their fine motor skills and spark their creativity. Many prompts in this book provide space for students to draw a picture alongside their written response.

Limit screen time.

For developing minds, the negative aspects associated with too much screen time are just beginning to be understood. Parents should set strict limits, particularly around bedtime.

TIPS FOR TEACHERS

Offer students lots of choices for reading, including both fiction and nonfiction.

Helping kids become lifelong readers is an essential goal in every classroom. Giving them choices helps build a love for books and language. The same goes for writing. Whenever possible, allow students to choose what they want to write about.

Practice makes perfect.

Kids in grades K-2 need to learn basic spelling, grammar, and writing mechanics. Teaching and testing these skills in Language Arts classes will help them become better readers and writers.

Give students regular chances to write.

You can add writing activities to arrival time or morning work. Use journals and set aside time two or three times a week for free writing. Have them write more formal, organized pieces after reading a book or finishing a unit.

Brag about your students.

Share, publish, and display good examples of student writing. Praise and recognition will encourage students more than a good grade.

Name: _____

 # FLOWERS

Fill in the sentences about flowers.

Use the word bank to write your answers below.

If I saw a

flower in a

I would give it to my   .

 Draw a picture of a flower.

Word Bank	
red	yellow
store	field
mom	teacher

11

Name: _____

MY DAD

What does your dad like to do?

Write your answer below.

exercise

go fishing

take a nap

watch TV

My dad likes to

_____ .

✎ *Draw a picture of your dad.*

Name: _____

MY MOM

What does your mom like to do?

Write your answer below.

exercise

read books

see friends

plant flowers

My mom likes to

_____

_____ •

✎ *Draw a picture of your mom.*

Name: _____

A BEE

Finish this poem with a word that rhymes.

I saw a bee

Up in a tree.

He was looking down at

                                                                    .

✏️ *Draw a picture of a bee in a tree.*

Word Bank
Dad
Mom
Me
grass
the ground

Name: _____

THE BEAR

Cut and paste the words to finish the story below.

A bear went into the   .

He saw some   .

"Yum!" he said. "I want

that   !"

school	forest
bees	cars
book	honey

15

Name: _____

DOG OR CAT?

Would you like to have a dog or a cat?

Cut out your answer and paste it into the sentence.

I want a

because they are

.

dog	cat
cute	fun
soft	playful

16

Name: _____

APPLES

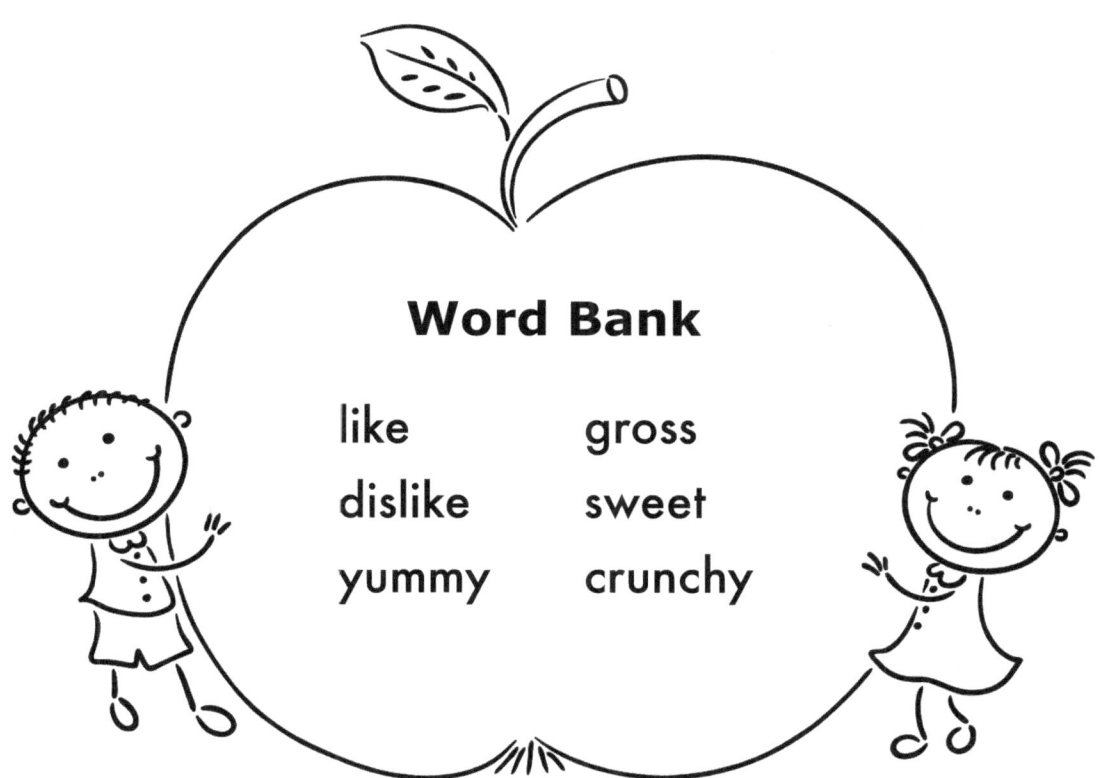

Word Bank

like	gross
dislike	sweet
yummy	crunchy

Do you like apples?

Use the word bank to write your answers below.

I _____ apples

because they are _____

_____ .

Name: _____

SHAPES

Describe the shapes.

Use the word bank to fill in the blanks.

 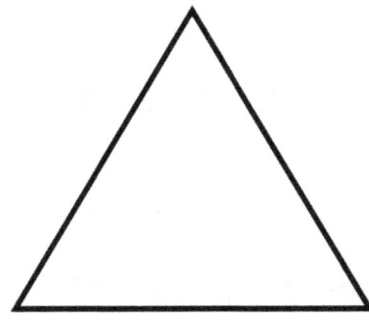 

The clock is   .

The triangle has   sides.

The star has   points.

Word Bank	
round	square
three	four
five	two

Name: _____

ALL ABOUT ME!

My name is _____.

I am _____ years old.

My hair is _____.

I like to _____.

Word Bank

five

six

black

brown

blonde

red

play video games

play outside

play with toys

read books

 Draw a picture of yourself.

Name: _____

MY TEACHER

What is your teacher like?

Write your answers below.

My teacher's name is

.

I think my teacher is

.

nice	smart	funny

I like it when my teacher

.

goes
outside

reads a
story

tells a joke

says, "Good
job!"

Name: _____

MY SCHOOL

Complete the sentences below.

My school's name is

•

In school, I like to

•

talk with
friends

read
stories

learn new
things

play on the
playground

The best part of school is

•

| making friends | playing games | eating lunch | learning |

DINOSAURS

Do you like dinosaurs?

Use the word bank to write your answers below.

I think dinosaurs are   .

If I saw a dinosaur, I would

                                                    •

✏ *Draw a picture of your favorite dinosaur.*

Word Bank	
cool	weird
scary	run
yell	say hello

Name: _____

ON A FARM

What do you see on a farm?

At a farm, there are

.

My favorite farm animal is a

.

 Draw a picture of your favorite farm animal.

Word Bank	
tractors	hay bales
barns	horse
chicken	cow

23

Name: _____

AT THE BEACH

What do you do at the beach?

| lie in the sun | build a sandcastle | look for shells | swim in the water |

At the beach, I like to

and

and

.

24

Name: _____

HAPPY BIRTHDAY!

Complete the sentences by matching them to the words and pictures.

On my birthday, I have a

fun

I invite my

party

We eat cake and

ice cream

Birthdays are

friends

25

Name: _____

AT THE PARK

What do you do at the park?

go down
slides

play on the
swings

ride my bike

play in the
sandbox

At the park, I like to

and

and

.

Name: _____

AT THE ZOO

What do you see at the zoo?

big animals

animals that hop

animals with spots

small animals

At the zoo, I see

and

and

.

Name: _____

LET'S COUNT!

Count the animals in the pictures. Finish the sentences.

I see

chickens.

I see

fish.

I see

cats.

Name: _____

RAINY DAYS

Complete the sentence below.

read books   watch TV   play with toys   play with friends

When it is raining, I like to

and

and

.

Name: _____

SUNNY DAYS

Complete the sentence below.

ride my
bike

go to the
playground

go swimming

play with
friends

When it is sunny, I like to

and

and

.

Name: _____

BABY BIRDS

Where do chicks come from? Cut and paste the words to complete the sentences.

First, the mother and father

birds make a   .

Next, they sit on the   .

Then, the eggs will   .

Out come the   !

| chicks | nest | eggs | hatch |

31

Name: _____

HOW TO GROW PLANTS

Cut and paste the words to finish the sentences below.

First, you plant the _____ .

Second, you give it _____ .

Next you put it in the _____ .

Last, you watch it _____ .

| sun | water | grow | seed |

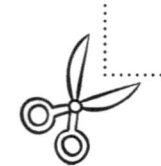

Name: _____

ICE CREAM

Use the word bank to complete the sentences below.

I eat ice cream in _____ .

My favorite flavor is _____

_____ •

I like it in a _____ .

 Draw a picture of your favorite ice cream treat.

Word Bank	
summer	winter
vanilla	chocolate
cone	dish

33

Name: _____

HOW TO BUILD A SNOWMAN

Use the word bank to fill in the blanks.

First, make a stack of three big

                                   .

Next, add   for arms.

Then, add a   as a nose.

Last, put a   on its head.

Word Bank	
snowballs	hat
sticks	bird
flowers	carrot

Name: _____

FOREST FRIENDS

Complete the sentences by matching them to the words and pictures.

An animal that has
antlers is a

An animal that has
red fur is a

fox

owl

An animal that has long
ears and hops is a

deer

An animal that lives in
trees and hoots is an

rabbit

Name: _____

CAN YOU FLY?

Finish this poem with a word that rhymes.

Can you fly?

You can try.

But only birds can reach the

.

Draw a picture of yourself flying.

Word Bank
air
sky
wings
ground

Name: _____

MY DOG

Finish this poem with a word that rhymes.

My dog is soft.

My dog is brown.

I always like when he's

_____ .

✏️ *Draw a picture of a dog.*

Word Bank
barking
asleep
around
hiding

37

Name: _____

FOUR SEASONS

Which season is your favorite? Finish the sentences below.

spring

summer

fall

winter

My favorite season is

because

and

Name: _____

MY CAT

Finish this poem with a word that rhymes.

Cats like to run.

Cats like to leap.

In the sun, cats like to

.

✏ *Draw a picture of a cat.*

Word Bank
stretch
sleep
drink
meow

Name: _____

I LOVE FALL

Complete the sentences by matching them to the words and pictures.

In the fall, my boots crunch the ....

leaves

I go back to

costume

I go to a farm and pick

school

I go trick-or-treating in a

pumpkins

40

Name: _____

GETTING TO SCHOOL

Word Bank

walking

carpool

bus

friends

early

fun

ride

How do you get to school?

Write about how you get to school. Use the word bank to help you.

I get to school by   .

I like it because

                                            .

Name: _____

NAME THE ANIMAL

Write the name of the animal under their picture.

Word Bank		
mouse	owl	deer
fish	fox	bear

Name: _____

MY FAVORITE SHOW

What is your favorite TV or YouTube show?

My favorite show is

because

Name: _____

I LOVE SCHOOL

What are three things you love about school?

First,	Second,	Third,

Name: _____

MY FAVORITE STORY

What is your favorite story?

My favorite story is

because

Name: _____

PLAYFUL PUPS

Pedro the pup meets a puppy named Penny. Write a fiction story about three things they do together.

First,	Next,	Last,

Name: _____

GETTING A PET

What pet would you get?

If I could have any pet, I would

get a

because

Name: _____

WHEN I GROW UP

What do you want to be when you grow up?

astronaut

doctor

teacher

musician

When I grow up, I want to be a

because

Name: _____

QUIET TIME

Name three things you can do during quiet time.

First,	Second,	Third,

Name: _____

YUM! YUM!

What do you like to eat?

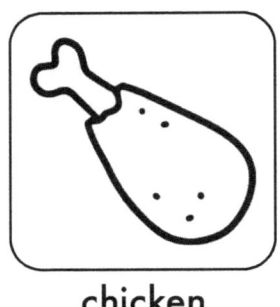   

chicken   french fries   ice cream   pizza

My favorite place to eat is

When I go there, I get

and

Name: _____

PLAY DATE

What do you do with your friends?

play games

play outside

play video games

play
hide-and-seek

When I have a play date, I like to

and

Name: _____

MY FAVORITE DAY

What is your favorite day of the week?

My favorite day of the week is

because

Name: _____

HELPING A FRIEND

How would you help a friend who feels sad?

If my friend is sad, I will help them by

Name: _____

LOST TOOTH

What happens when you lose a tooth?

First,

_____

_____

Then,

_____

_____

Last,

_____

_____

Name: _____

WHICH ONE?

Would you rather be a bee or a giraffe?

I would be a

because

Name: _____

LIONS AND TIGERS

How are lions and tigers the same? How are they different?

Same:

Different:

Name: _____

THREE WISHES

If a genie granted you three wishes, what would you wish for?

First,

Second,

Third,

Name: _____

WHEN I'M ANGRY

What do you do when you get angry?

make a craft

play a sport

read a book

play music

When I get angry, I

because it helps me

Name: _____

MOVIES OR PARK?

Would you rather go to the movies or the park?

I would rather go to the

because

Name: _____

RECESS!

What do you like most about recess?

I think recess is

I like it because

Name: _____

LETTER TO MOM

Draw a picture of your mom and write her a letter.

Dear Mom,

Name: _____

OUTDOOR FUN

Name three things you like to do outside.

First,

Second,

Third,

Name: _____

IN A SUBMARINE

Would you like to ride in a submarine?

Riding in a submarine would

be

because

GETTING READY FOR BED

Here is how I get ready for bed.

First,	Next,	Last,

Name: _____

LOST KITTEN

What would you do if you found a lost kitten?

If I found a lost kitten, I would

Then, I would

Name: _____

GOING TO A PICNIC

What would you bring to a picnic?

If I went to a picnic, I would bring
and

Name: _____

GRANDMA'S HOUSE

What do you do at your grandma's house?

I like going to Grandma's house because

Name: _____

LET IT SNOW!

What do you like to do in the snow?

snowman

skating

sledding

skiing

When it snows outside, I

and

and

Name: _____

AT THE POND

What do you see and do at the pond?

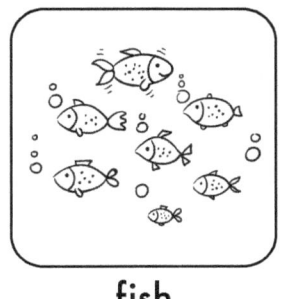

fish

duck

turtle

boat

I like visiting the pond because

and

and

Name: _____

A NEW BIKE

What would you do with a new bike?

First,	Next,	Then,

Name: _____

MOON POEM

Use the word bank to help you finish the poem with rhyming words.

The moon comes out at

It shines so

It looks almost

The moon is quite a

Word Bank: face, bright, white, light, rock, night, sight

71

Name: _____

THANK YOU LETTER

Write a thank-you letter to someone.

Dear

Thank you for

Sincerely,

(Write your name here.)

Name: _____

OPINION: SCHOOL

What do you like best about school?

I like

and

Name: _____

DOLPHINS AND SHARKS

How are dolphins and sharks the same? How are they different?

Same:

Different:

Name: _____

MY FAVORITE HOLIDAY

What is your favorite holiday?

Christmas

Easter

Fourth of July

Halloween

My favorite holiday is

I like it because

and

Name: _____

MY BUS DRIVER IS AN ALIEN!

Imagine your new bus driver is an alien. Finish the story below describing your ride to school.

When the bus arrived this morning, I was surprised to see...

Name: _____

FEELING PROUD

Write about a time when you felt proud of yourself.

I felt proud when I

_____

_____

_____

I learned

_____

_____

_____

_____

_____

_____

_____

Name: _____

I CAN BE HEALTHY

How do you stay healthy?

exercise

sleep

food

water

It's important to stay healthy because

_____

_____

Here are three things I do to keep healthy:

First,	Second,	Third,

Name: _____

FARM ANIMAL POEM

Write an acrostic poem about a farm animal. Use at least 15 words in your poem. Here is an example:

Pink pigs are having fun
In the mud, they roll around
Getting cool
Smart but smelly animals

Now it's your turn!

Name: _____

MY FAVORITE HOBBY

What is your favorite hobby?

riding my bike

fishing

reading

cooking

My favorite hobby is
_____

Here are three reasons I like this hobby:

First,	Second,	Third,

Name: _____

MEETING A FAMOUS PERSON

What famous person do you want to meet?

I would love to meet

I want to meet this person because

I would ask them

Draw a picture of the person you want to meet.

Name: _____

SWEET OR SALTY?

Do you like sweet or salty snacks best?

I like _____

_____

_____

_____

because _____

_____

_____

_____

_____

_____

_____

Name: _____

ROBOT TEACHER

Imagine your new teacher is a robot named Robert. Write a fictional story about your first day with your new teacher.

When I entered the classroom, I was surprised

to see...

Draw a picture of your new robot teacher.

Name: _____

OPINION: DOGS AT SCHOOL

Should dogs be allowed at school? List three reasons why you think dogs should or should not be allowed at school.

First,

_____

_____

_____

Second,

_____

_____

_____

Third,

_____

_____

_____

Name: _____

MY FRIEND AND ME

How are you and your best friend alike? How are you different?

Same	Different

Name: _____

ROAD TRIP!

Write about the last time you went on a road trip.

On this trip, I went to

_____

_____

_____

I went with

_____

_____

_____

This trip was fun because

_____

_____

_____

Name: _____

SNOW DAY!

Imagine a snowstorm hits your town, and you have no school for a day. How would you spend your day?

First, _____

_____

_____

Next, _____

_____

_____

Last, _____

_____

_____

Name: _____

BEES AND BUTTERFLIES

How are bees and butterflies alike? How are they different?

Same	Different

Name: _____

A TALKING BEAR

Write a fictional story about a child named J.J. who meets a talking bear.

One day, J.J. walked into her backyard and saw a bear sitting in the grass. The bear said, "

Draw a picture of J.J. and the bear.

Name: _____

MY GARDEN

Imagine you have a big garden ready to be planted. Using full sentences, write about three things you would plant in your garden.

First,

Second,

Third,

Draw a picture of your garden.

Name: _____

WRAPPING A GIFT

How do you wrap a gift? Write the steps in the boxes below.

First,	Second,	Third,

✏️ *Draw a picture of your gift.*

Name: _____

FIRST DAY OF SCHOOL

What was your first day of second grade like?

On the first day of second grade, I felt

My teacher was

By the end of the day,

Name: _____

CAR OR AIRPLANE?

If you have to take a long trip, would you rather take a car or an airplane?

 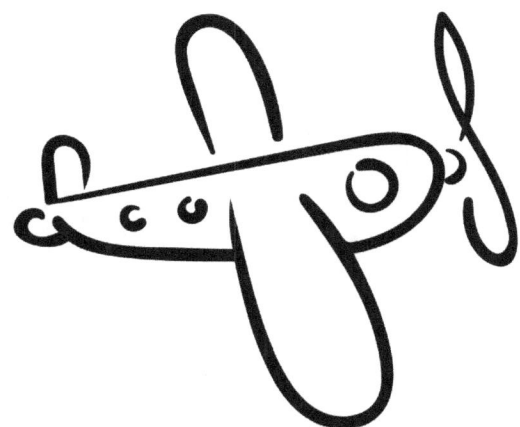

I would rather take

_____

_____

_____

because

_____

_____

_____

_____

_____

_____

_____

Name: _____

CAMPING TRIP

What things do you take camping?

When I go camping, I take

_____

_____

and

_____

_____

and

_____

_____

Name: _____

PARK OR FRIEND?

Would you rather spend the afternoon at the park or with a friend?

I would rather spend the afternoon

_____

_____

because

_____

_____

_____

_____

_____

Name: _____

MISSING PET POSTER

Draw a missing pet poster. Add the pet's picture and a description of what they look like. Include your name and phone number so people can contact you.

MISSING

Pet's name:

Who to contact:

Description:

Phone number:

Name: _____

GETTING READY FOR SCHOOL

How do you get ready for school in the morning?

First,
_____
_____
_____

Next,
_____
_____
_____

Last,
_____
_____
_____

Name: _____

BEACH ADVENTURE

Finish the story below about an unusual day at the beach.

At the beach one afternoon, I found...

Draw a picture of your unusual beach discovery.

Name: _____

THE DRAGON

Write a fictional story about meeting a dragon.

I found a cave and went inside to explore.

There was a dragon! Then...

Name: _____

THE AMUSEMENT PARK

What do you do at an amusement park?

When I go to an amusement park...

_____

_____

_____

_____

_____

_____

_____

_____

_____

_____

_____

Name: _____

MY FEELINGS

How do you manage your feelings?

When I am sad, I

_____

_____

When I am happy, I

_____

_____

When I am scared, I

_____

_____

Name: _____

THE BEST DAY EVER

Write about your best day ever.

My best day ever was when

It was the best because:

First,	Second,	Third,

Name: _____

MY FAVORITE MOVIE

What is your favorite movie?

My favorite movie is

It is about

I like it because

Name: _____

I HAVE MONEY!

What would you do with $100?

If I had $100, I would

_____

_____

_____

After that,

_____

_____

_____

Finally,

_____

_____

_____

Name: _____

OUTER SPACE

Would you go to outer space?

If I had the chance to go to space, I

because

Name: _____

A SCREEN-FREE DAY

Imagine you cannot use any screens for an entire day. What would you do all day?

On a screen-free day, I would...

Draw a picture of a screen-free activity.

Name: _____

AN UNUSUAL DREAM

Have you had a weird dream? Write down what happened.

First, _____

_____

_____

Then, _____

_____

_____

Last, _____

_____

_____

_____

Name: _____

WOULD YOU RATHER

Would you rather be a squirrel or a fish?

I would rather be a

because

Draw yourself as a squirrel or a fish.

Name: _____

LIZARD OR BIRD?

Would you rather have a lizard or a bird for a pet?

I would rather have

_____

_____

_____

because

_____

_____

_____

_____

_____

_____

ABOUT THE AUTHOR

MARK TREVOR has been a language arts teacher for nearly 25 years and has taught students from kindergarten through grade 12. He currently lives in Cary, North Carolina.